THIS IS
WHAT
I KNOW
ABOUT ART

KIMBERLY DREW

PENGUIN WORKSHOP

Thank you to my family for raising me to be the best version
of myself. None of my accomplishments would be possible
without a childhood bathed in love and encouragement.
And thank you to my friends for taking the baton and running
with me full speed into a more loving, beautiful future.
I would be nothing without each and every one of you—KD

PENGUIN WORKSHOP
An Imprint of Penguin Random House LLC, New York

Penguin supports copyright. Copyright fuels creativity, encourages diverse voices,
promotes free speech, and creates a vibrant culture. Thank you for buying an authorized
edition of this book and for complying with copyright laws by not reproducing, scanning,
or distributing any part of it in any form without permission. You are supporting writers
and allowing Penguin to continue to publish books for every reader.

The publisher does not have any control over and does not assume any responsibility for
author or third-party websites or their content.

Text copyright © 2020 by Kimberly Drew. Illustrations copyright © 2020 by
Penguin Random House LLC. All rights reserved. Published by Penguin Workshop,
an imprint of Penguin Random House LLC, New York. PENGUIN and
PENGUIN WORKSHOP are trademarks of Penguin Books Ltd, and the W colophon
is a registered trademark of Penguin Random House LLC. Manufactured in China.

Visit us online at www.penguinrandomhouse.com.

Library of Congress Cataloging-in-Publication Data is available upon request.

ISBN 9780593095188   10 9 8 7 6 5 4 3 2 1

PROLOGUE

Thank you for choosing this book. Whether you're at the checkout of your favorite store, in transit, or you graciously accepted this book as a gift—I'm glad that you've opened it and are taking a chance on something new. Books can be intimidating. They might be fun to look at, but reading and digesting a text can be tough. Like change or progress, reading takes time. So whether you read straight through or pick this book up here or there, I'm excited to be in conversation with you.

In all honesty, I never thought that I'd write anything that would find an audience. For most of my life, I thought that the written word, especially books about art, could be written only by scholars and people with fancy doctoral degrees. The truth is: We all have the power to engage with and write about art.

I had ambitions to present a broad lesson on art history and protest, but as I began my research, that felt disingenuous. I revisited writings by art historians Lucy Lippard and Susan Cahan, among others, but I wanted to talk about my own journey with art. I'm not your typical art historian. I am not your typical activist. I am still learning what art and protest mean to me. And so, this book is more about my journey through art toward activism. This book is about discovery, confusion, and progress.

Simply, I want to share my stories with the hope that you may find your own journey and make the changes that you want to see in the world.

As I write this book, organizers are staging boycotts of museums and art programs worldwide. People are fighting for equal pay, demanding changes in leadership, and so much more. We are in the middle of a hot, fiery mess, and I don't think anyone currently working in the field has the solutions to resolve any of these issues easily.

Art and protest will forever be bound together. And the beautiful thing about art, like activism, is that it allows us space to be curious and learn. Sharing art has helped me learn how to make my voice heard and ask better questions.

If being in the arts has taught me anything, it is that one of the wisest things anyone can say is "I don't know."

This book is about what I do know.

THIS IS WHAT I KNOW ABOUT ART

My first art-related memory (as told by my mother) is from kindergarten. From a very young age, I have known "my lane." When assigned art projects, I would trade my lunch for artwork made by my classmates who I knew had better art skills. Why make my own drawings when I knew someone who could do it better? I like to think of kindergarten as my first workshop in art activism: I refused my teacher's expectations, turning instead to my immediate community of peers so that I would not have to perform labor I had no interest in performing.

This is not to say I did not love art or expression from a young age. Growing up, I loved visiting art spaces. I enjoyed the sense of calm in each gallery.

My father's two sisters instilled a love of fine art in me, and during family gatherings, visiting a museum would usually be on the itinerary. My mother's brother DJ'd in the 1970s and 1980s, and my godmother went to the Boston Conservatory at Berklee. Art and self-expression were essential pillars in my childhood. But, even with early exposure to art and art spaces, I never would have dared to dream about working in the arts in the capacity that I do now. Art was always in the background, but it wasn't until my sophomore year of college that working in the arts felt like a possibility for me.

Unlike my first year, my second year at Smith College didn't start with excitement about classes or hanging out in the Campus Center; it started with a rigorous campaign at Smith's Office of Student Financial Services. I was depressed, burned-out, and I felt like I was failing in every direction. I'd had my heart broken for the first time that summer by my first girlfriend, and my grades were terrible. I had been working so hard to be admitted to an elite college, but in my first year I felt like I was wasting my opportunity. I'd spent my high school years at an elite boarding school feeling like the beneficiary of affirmative action, and while I knew I had potential, my grades were lackluster and an unwelcome reminder of my insecurities.

On top of my heartbreak, my grandfather passed away my first year of college, and while we were never close, his death had a tremendous impact on my financial aid package. My immediate family did not inherit any money, but the federal government thought otherwise. This nightmare, one experienced by so many families trying to pay for college, only worsened when I couldn't enroll in classes for the fall semester due to financial holds on my account. I took on the maximum number of work-study hours and petitioned for a private loan to support myself.

It was a privilege to have been admitted to Smith, but it was a struggle to maintain my dignity when I trudged uphill from the quad toward that financial services office every morning to plead my case for additional funding.

My education came at a high price—an emotional one and a monetary one.

That December, my academic adviser, Kevin E. Quashie, recommended that I apply for a summer internship at the Studio Museum in Harlem, a museum dedicated to showing art by people of the African diaspora, or the Schomburg Center for Research in Black Culture at the New York Public Library. Up until that point, I'd pinballed among several possible majors, studying mathematics, chemistry, engineering, and architecture (even though I hate to draw). I thought I *needed* to be a doctor or engineer after graduating from school. I was smart and I knew I needed to turn that intelligence into revenue, but the only classes I enjoyed were in the African American Studies department. For so many young people of color, we feel like we don't have the luxury of exploring the liberal arts—society tells us that we have to take coursework to become high earners to make valuable contributions to the world.

I can't remember if I applied to both the Studio Museum and the Schomburg, but I know that I confidently applied to the Studio Museum because its internship was paid.[1] It's absurd to think about how a $1,600 stipend changed the course of my life. It's absurd to think about how many internships are *still* unpaid, and how elitist and morally corrupt it is to hire unpaid or underpaid labor.

When I was accepted to the program, I was shocked. I had only taken one art history class (a survey of Asian art), but I was thrilled by the opportunity to see how the discipline was practiced in the real world.

(We talk about "impostor syndrome," or the feeling that you don't belong somewhere. Then and now, I dismiss feelings of impostor syndrome. How can there be one diagnosis for an anxiety that feels so tailored to who you are as a person?)

As a former math major, I did the calculations: I was not confident enough, polished enough, or *anything* enough to have been selected. Everything I knew about myself reminded me that I was, if not an impostor, a fraud. As I nervously walked down

1. I applied to the Studio Museum only because its internship was paid. I wonder how many young people don't apply to internships because they are unpaid.

125th Street for my first day, I was sure that someone had made a mistake. I recalled the grandness of Duke Ellington's "Take the A Train" rendition, which explored the journey from Brooklyn to Harlem in the 1930s. I thought of the YouTube videos I would constantly watch of Ellington masterfully playing the keys. I daydreamed about the Harlem Renaissance and knew that I was surely not the second coming of Josephine Baker or Zora Neale Hurston.

When I'd gotten off the A train, I'd found myself walking behind a tall, Afroed Black woman, who I'd later learn was the museum's associate curator, Naomi Beckwith. There were merchants on every corner, some with red, black, and green versions of the American flag. You could hear drum circles playing in the Adam Clayton Powell plaza, or hip-hop blasting from boom boxes on vendors' tables. There's a sonic quality to 125th Street that I can't quite explain. Despite the bombastic soundscape of each block, the sounds never conflicted. The synergy was otherworldly. I kept a safe distance observing her stride—envying the confidence in her movement. Her back was straight, upright, her dark-washed denim jeans tailored to perfection. She could have just as easily been strutting down a runway in Milan or Paris. Following this goddess distracted me from my nervousness until she turned to enter the museum's red lobby.

The lobby wasn't grand or glamorous, but it was where everyone began their journey into the museum. It was where I arrived, it was where every staff member arrived, and it was also where every VIP guest would find themselves at one point during their visit. To your right, there was the ticket desk, usually manned by a gentleman named Timothy with a commanding baritone voice and a serene, ballerina-like posture. To your left, you could see a neon piece by the artist Glenn Ligon that would flash *Me* or *We*. The work, called *Give Us a Poem (Palindrome #2)*, was inspired by Muhammad Ali's 1975 visit to Harvard University where he was asked to improvise a poem during a question and answer session. Ali replied, "Me/We," a poem that doubly spoke to solidarity and difference. The museum became my home for ten glorious weeks.

As part of the internship, we went on field trips, met with art leaders, and had time to explore the galleries. It was so exciting to me that I could walk downstairs from our office and be immersed in one of the world's best collections of art by Black artists.

One day, while on a break, I discovered a black-and-white photograph of the artist Andy Warhol and a Black friend wearing boxing gloves and boxing shorts. I knew a little bit about Andy Warhol, but wondered who this beautiful Black person standing next to him could be. Their gloves lightly touched and the Black subject's locs sat up like a crown on his head. After reading more about the image, I learned the other man in the portrait was Jean-Michel Basquiat. Curious about his connection, I googled "Jean-Michel Basquiat," and with each page of search results, I found dynamic, extraordinary paintings that fused text and image. I thought, *I've found the Black Warhol!* Then, it occurred to me: How did I know about Andy Warhol and not know about "the Black Warhol"?

Where had this information been hiding? How many more Black versions of my favorite artists were there? (Jean-Michel Basquiat is absolutely not "the Black Warhol"—as I naively thought—nor are there "Black versions" of non-Black artists. He was an artist in his own lane, much like the other people that I'll reference throughout the rest of this book. The names you'll read here are all carefully selected to guide, educate, and inform you. If you read the name of an artist or other person that you don't know, I hope you'll take frequent pauses to research them.)

When the internship ended, I added Trenton Doyle Hancock, Lorna Simpson, and Glenn Ligon to the list of Black artists that I knew. I began to realize that there were so many dynamic Black artists who worked as painters, photographers, and performers. There was a whole Black world that I knew almost nothing about. I needed to know more. I'd gained a clarity that I'd never had before. Moreover, I was assured that I needed to work in museums. The Studio Museum had taken a chance on me, and I wanted to take a chance on the art world.

I was on a mission. When I got back to Smith College, I dropped my architecture major and began to register for art history classes. Because I was a junior, I had to take three art history classes a semester to complete the major. Though determined, I was also working two jobs and knew almost nothing about art. I could feel myself shrink as my classmates would answer questions about Baroque art with ease. I worked tirelessly to keep up with my peers.

As time went on, I also realized that I didn't get many opportunities to learn about the artists and movements that got me interested in art in the first place. There have been Black people since the beginning of time, but I was not seeing any of their art in any of my classes. How would I find more artists like Basquiat, Hancock, Simpson, or Ligon?

I took to the internet to find resources that I could use to continue the lessons that began at the Studio Museum. I searched and searched but did not find anything worthwhile. After a few months of research, I decided that I should start my own blog. (I am still at a loss for where I got the confidence to do so, but I am forever grateful to the version of myself that said yes. Yes to learning more about Black art. Yes to making the things that I knew I needed to see in the world.)

At the time, I also discovered writings by Carter G. Woodson, the founder of Negro History Week, which would later grow to become Black History Month. He wrote that "If a race has no history, it has no worthwhile tradition, it becomes a negligible factor in the thought of the world, and it stands in danger of being exterminated." I did not want Black art to be a negligible factor. I did not want Black art to be exterminated. I saw it happening in my art history classes, and I just had to do something to build a history online.[2] I reached out to a few friends, and on March 2, 2011, Black Contemporary Art on Tumblr was born. First, I started posting about artists that I'd already learned of: Jamel Shabazz, then Samuel Fosso, Nick Cave, and Mickalene Thomas. Those names felt like a good start. Then I widened my search—I reposted a picture of Stephen Wiltshire, a British autistic artist who can draw entire cities from memory.

2. It's important to note that I was twenty years old and thought that information began and ended on the internet.

For the next few months, I obsessed over finding new artists to add to the site. The blog's editorial team grew by two volunteers, Coco Lopez and Geraldine Richards. Having a team meant that every day there was a possibility for discovery—for us and for our audience. It was and is the product of our collective hard work.

I posted every two hours around the clock. Some friends were worried about the hours I kept as I worked. I searched museum websites, other Tumblrs, and any resource that I could find to add more art to the blog. I knew that I wanted to record as many Black artists as possible for anyone, like me, who needed to see more art by Black people. I knew that I had to resist the erasure of Black artists. I did not want anyone to say that Black artists did not exist.

In the second semester of my junior year, I was finally able to enroll in a lecture on modern and contemporary art.

I was hype. I'd covered what I had assumed were the basics: I had learned about buildings all over Italy and done research papers on the Dutch Masters. I was ready to study contemporary art, a field that I thought would be more representative of my interests. Lecture after lecture and week after week, I would diligently research the names that we'd learned—hoping, praying that some of them would be the names of Black people. It feels silly now, but I remember thinking that Adolph Gottlieb must be Black. His *Pictographs* paintings were reminiscent of African masks, but it turns out that Gottlieb was just another white art dude, and, according to the Guggenheim Museum website, if "Gottlieb discovered that a symbol had a recognizable meaning within either Western or tribal art, he immediately removed it from his painting vocabulary as part of his quest for a collective unconscious." By the third or fourth week of class, I wanted to remove much of what we had learned from my own vocabulary.

That was, until the day we learned about Cuban American artist Coco Fusco and Chicano performance artist Guillermo Gómez-Peña.

The lecture started like any other, but instead of a slideshow, our professor showed Fusco and Gómez-Peña's 1993 documentary *The Couple in the Cage*. The film followed Fusco and Gómez-Peña on their tour of *The Couple in the Cage: Two Undiscovered Amerindians Visit the West*, a performance art piece that mimicked the colonial tradition of presenting "savage," "native," or otherwise "foreign" people for consumption by white audiences at world's fairs. While the performances started as a commentary on the tradition of this display, the audience immediately believed that Fusco and Gómez-Peña were *actually* "Amerindians" from the Gulf of Mexico. The piece's satirical nature was completely lost, and during interviews after the performance, visitors explained their ridiculous theories about the two performers.

When the video ended, our professor opened the floor for dialogue, but instead of an enlightening conversation about the art piece itself, there was an emotional reaction from some of my white classmates. The discussion began with anger and discomfort, and then a chorus of white guilt[3] and tears erupted. Some students were upset by the artists' intention, and others were ashamed of the history that the piece highlighted. I, on the other hand, felt solidarity with the artists' need to highlight the shameful history of the world's fair and how, more often than not, people of color are brought into art spaces to perform for

3. "White guilt is a culturally and historically contingent emotion rooted in White people's recognition of unearned privileges and collective and/or individual roles in the perpetuation of racism." Patrick R. Grzanka, "White Guilt: Race, Gender, Sexuality and Emergent Racisms in the Contemporary United States," Dissertation, Digital Repository at the University of Maryland: 2010.

white audiences. How couldn't my classmates see beyond their guilt?

Two days later we returned to class, and before we could continue talking about *The Couple in the Cage*, our professor cold-opened with the words "If I were an African American, I would see white guilt as equally as offensive as outright racism." My entire body jerked. After class, I took to Facebook to tell my story. I wrote: "[Redacted]'s first words at 10:30am were 'if i were an african american . . .'" I knew that he was trying to remedy the divide in our classroom, but something in his language didn't sit well with me. Why would he have to "be an African American" to see that this guilt was monopolizing the conversation?

By the end of the week, I got a vague email requesting my presence at his office hours.

That afternoon, I waited in Hillyer Art Library, working on the Black Contemporary Art blog. I posted a quote by the scholar bell hooks that explained: "Throughout African American history, performance has been crucial in the struggle for liberation, precisely because it has not required the material resources demanded by other art forms." I was ready for an ideological discussion about performance art in Black culture. I was ready to defend my Facebook post, too.

When our meeting began, the professor noted that it was inappropriate for me to have taken his quote out of context. I had walked into his office ready for a debate, but I could see his point. Perhaps I had been too harsh. Was I bullying him?

Then, just as I began to regret the post, he went on to explain that I had also made my classmates feel "uncomfortable" during the discussion. I retorted, explaining that I was upset the conversation had quickly turned into a support circle for white guilt. He looked at me and said, "If you wanted to be in a classroom with other students of color then you should not have enrolled in art history classes."

This professor was my art history adviser.

In my life, I have made a point of telling stories of triumph. I have had to fight so many battles to succeed that I want to maintain an agency with how my story is told. I never want my story to be defined by a string of heartbreaks, but that exchange with my adviser marked me forever. It made me feel alone. It almost broke me.

In "The Other History of Intercultural Performance," Coco Fusco recounts the impact of performing *The Couple in the Cage*, explaining:

> *The memory of [an] ethnographic filmmaker's gaze haunted me for years, to the point that I began to wonder if I had become paranoid . . . Those are the moments when I am glad that there are real bars there. Those are also the times when, even though I know I can get out of the cage, I can never quite escape.*

When I graduated from school, I also wanted an escape. I was able to walk for graduation, even though I still owed the college $400, and I didn't receive my diploma until later that summer. Receiving an empty diploma booklet was a welcome metaphor for how much work I still had to do. I was paranoid, but at least I knew my next step. That June, I began a paid fellowship at Creative Time, a public art organization based in New York City. Growing up in New Jersey, I hated the idea of moving to New York. I wanted to travel far beyond the comforts of the East Coast, but I could not say no to a paying gig (even if it paid poorly).

When I applied to work at Creative Time, I did not know much about its history, but its mission felt like a good fit. Creative Time centers on three core values: "Art matters, artists' voices are important in shaping society, and public spaces are places for creative and free expression." Shortly after arriving, I learned about projects including *Tribute in Light*, the twin beacons of light that illuminated Lower Manhattan just months after 9/11, and Gran Fury's *Kissing Doesn't Kill: Greed and Indifference Do*, an installation that manipulated media and advertising to shed light on the AIDS crisis.

Each week at Creative Time, I sifted through the organization's archives, learning about the work of artists including Marlon Riggs, Karen Finley, Marilyn Minter, Jenny Holzer, and Félix González-Torres.

González-Torres took my breath away. I was struck by his use of everyday objects. In *Untitled (Perfect Lovers)*, he programmed two battery-powered, synchronized clocks (that kind of looked like the clocks you might see in a public school or doctor's office). González-Torres made the piece while his partner, Ross Laycock, was losing a battle with AIDS-related illness from 1987 to 1990. It was the most romantic artwork I had ever seen. In an interview, González-Torres shared, "I don't want to make art just for people who can read Fredric Jameson sitting upright on a Mackintosh chair. I want to make art for people who watch *The Golden Girls* and sit in a big, brown La-Z-Boy chair. They're part of my public too, I hope." The burgeoning art nerd in me fell in love with González-Torres's ability to fuse the personal and political. He made conceptual art about love and loss for all of us. His pieces helped me think about how I could bring tenderness to my work and that I didn't have to divorce myself from my own identity.

Though I appreciated my fellowship, I could not help but be frustrated by my environment. When I was hired, I was one of five people of color in our office. Two of us were on temporary fellowships, two were unpaid interns, and one of us was working full-time as a curatorial assistant. This meant that the only person of color on staff was likely earning one of the lowest salaries on the curatorial team, if not within the entire organization. It was a distracting disparity, to say the least.

When I wasn't at work or hustling to art events for free food, I continued to cultivate my blog. It was my refuge.

The more art I saw, the more I wanted to share it with others. My Instagram account, which had once been a site for overly edited selfies, became an opportunity to introduce my audience to everything that I was discovering. Back then, I remember thinking how implausible it was that I was working at Creative Time, and, more specifically, how inconceivable it was that a young Black person from New Jersey was being invited into such an exclusive world. I decided that

I could use my Instagram to illustrate my success, despite the odds. Maybe people would think, *If they can do it, so can I.*

I developed a system: I'd visit as many shows as possible, and I'd post one to three images from each show. I made a point of focusing on exhibitions in the Chelsea neighborhood of New York, because all of those exhibitions were free to the public (and at that time I never had more than about sixty dollars in my bank account). I thought that if people knew shows were free, they might go visit them.

In the spring of 2013, I was thrilled when the exhibition *Blues for Smoke* traveled from the Museum of Contemporary Art, Los Angeles to the Whitney Museum of American Art in New York. *Blues for Smoke* looked at the function of the blues as a form of cultural expression through the lens of contemporary art. The artists in the show represented different races, but there were several artists I'd studied for my blog. Bennett Simpson, the exhibition curator, said, ". . . the blues is about anticipation," and I could not wait to experience so many works mounted in real life by artists that I'd only known through JPEGs. More importantly, I also really wanted to make sure that as many Black people as possible went to see the show.

With this goal in mind, I collaborated with Alie Cline, the founder of the Tumblr blog Cave to Canvas, to lead an "art walk." We reached out to Tumblr's Arts Evangelist, Annie Werner, to pitch the idea for an art tour, and coordinated a free daylong event to see *Blues for Smoke* at the Whitney and James Turrell's *Roden Crater and Autonomous Structures* at Pace Gallery's Midtown location.

The art walk was a total dream. I had been a huge fan of Alie's blog, and it was surreal to have Tumblr's support. At the time, I remember thinking that people may need more personal invitations to visit exhibitions. I felt that a human element was missing. I wanted to deliver as many invitations as possible— digitally and in person.

A few weeks after the art walk, I was excited to take my mom to see *Blues for Smoke*, too. It meant the world to be able to guide her through the Whitney and rave to her about the Black artists on view. I had been out of college for just under a year and was really starting to feel grounded in the art world. I wanted to invite her to see the arts through this new lens.

During our visit, I raved about Rodney McMillian's red leather chapel installation, and paintings by Alma Thomas and Kerry James Marshall, and I gleefully shared my affection for the director, Wu Tsang. I wanted to make as many connections as possible for my mom in an effort to guide her experience. We observed Zoe Leonard's *1961*—a conceptual self-portrait featuring a series of suitcases that represented each year of her life. The works in the show were all so personal, and relaying all of those narratives felt like an opportunity to introduce these artists as heroes to my mother.

When my rapid-fire tour of *Blues for Smoke* ended, we visited another floor to view works from the museum's permanent collection. Before we left the building, I wanted to take her to see some artwork that I thought she might know. We rounded a corner and I pointed to a work by Andy Warhol, assuming that my mother was somewhat familiar with his work, too. She said she did not know who he was and that she had not been in a museum since I'd been born. Time stopped. Growing up, I had always visited museums with my dad and his sisters, but I never thought about the fact that my mom was never there.

I do not remember much about the rest of the visit, or what happened after we left the museum, but I will never forget that moment. Engaging with my brilliant mother in a space from which, for whatever reason, she had been excluded complicated the way that I viewed art museums. On one hand, I immediately realized that my mother was part of a majority of Black people who do not frequent museums. She'd always been a member of the audience I yearned to invite into the art world. On the other hand, my mother had lived for more than two decades without a visit to a museum, and it seemingly had little impact on her life. I had so many questions. Why hadn't she been to a museum? Did she even want to visit them?

What *do* museums even *do*? I'd been working so diligently to get Black people into museums that I had never stopped to think about what would happen if we did not want to be there.

I was twenty-three years old when I returned to the Studio Museum to manage their social media. It was my dream job, and I took it very seriously. I knew how to write a great tweet, but the job description did not begin to cover the amount of work I'd be doing. I learned how to run the museum's social media, manage interns, use Adobe InDesign, update the website, and basically do any other task that came across my desk.

Real talk—working at a small and under-resourced art institution was a powerful, humbling experience.

On social media, I aimed to connect the burgeoning #BlackTwitter community to Black art. My primary strategy was to use it to entice Black audiences to come to the museum. On Instagram, I used pictures of our guests in the gallery to show our audience that they might see themselves there, too. I knew the power of representation and tried to leverage the image in a way that felt authentic. With each post, I tried to channel Timothy, who worked at the front desk, or Ms. Lisa, who guarded the galleries. How would everyday people invite visitors into an art experience? How might that gesture be performed digitally? Social media could be so cold, and I wanted to make it warmer for our prospective guests.

During the first few months of my work at the Studio Museum, our numbers grew. I'd gone from fraud to peacock. I thought I knew it all. I let that cockiness get the best of me when the Whitney Museum announced its artists list for the 2014 Whitney Biennial. Every two years, the Whitney Museum hosts an epic exhibition that features the artistic talent it believes defines "art today." It's one of those shows that can totally jump-start your career. Of the 103 artists selected for the exhibition that year, only nine were Black. And, as if to add insult to injury, the curatorial committee invited the white male artist Joe Scanlan to be in the biennial under the pseudonym of Donelle Woolford, a fictional Black woman artist who was brought to life by Black women actresses on Joe's payroll. There is significant literature available that painstakingly explains this work as a continuation of the minstrel show tradition, the racist performance of blackface which lampoons Black life for white audiences. The news shot through our offices. It was racist, hurtful, and anti-Black. With my then supervisor's permission, I posted a piece by the Guerrilla Girls to the Studio Museum's Tumblr page in protest of Scanlan's inclusion and the exclusion of so many POC artists that I knew deserved to be in the exhibition.

The Guerrilla Girls is an anonymous artist collective that was founded in the mid-1980s to be the conscience for the art world. In 1995, they made a piece called *Traditional Values and Quality Return to the Whitey Museum*, in response to the biennial artist lists from 1991 to 1995. The 1993 biennial had been the museum's most diverse biennial to date and had also received an overwhelming volume of criticism. In 1995, the curatorial team significantly reduced the percentage of marginalized artists. (The Guerrilla Girls say that when they tried to write about this change and typeset *Whitney*, they couldn't find the letter *n*. Hence, "the Whitey Museum.") The percentages for the 1995 biennial were not too different from those for 2014—so we posted it.

But I didn't stop there. On my own social media pages, I wrote angry tweets about the lack of diversity, and by the end of the weekend, I had fielded interviews with a local art blog and *The Huffington Post*. By Monday, word had gotten back to the Studio Museum, and yet again I was called into a superior's office for something that I'd shared on social media. This time, though, the stakes were higher. This time, it was the director's office. Thelma Golden's office, to be exact. Golden, who had also graduated from Smith College, is one of the most important curators in the history of art. Her exhibitions, including *Black Male*; *Freestyle*; the 1993 Whitney Biennial; and my personal favorite, *harlemworld*, changed the language that we use when we talk and/or think about identity. She was not just my boss. She is *the* boss.

During my meeting with Thelma, she told me about the consequences of my actions and generously taught me that my voice was a powerful one. Instead of leading with rage, she helped me understand this difficult crossroads. By the end of the meeting, she asked me to think deeply about what I wanted to say, and, more importantly, how I wanted it to be interpreted. It was not just enough to be angry. I had to be strategic.

After a year at the Studio Museum, I left to take a new job as an assistant at a privately owned art gallery.

I was excited about the new job, but it was remarkably different from life in Harlem. I had never worked in the for-profit world. When I started at the gallery, Mickalene Thomas's exhibition *Tête de Femme* was on view. The walls of the gallery were covered with grand, abstract paintings that brilliantly gleaned inspiration from Édouard Manet, Henri Matisse, and Romare Bearden. The *Femme* portraits were quite different from her earlier works, which were usually more representational. In each of these mosaic-like works, Thomas seemed to be pushing the limits of what her audience expected of her. Each canvas was a refusal of the way that she'd been known as an artist. It was a new beginning for her practice. Perhaps it was a new beginning for the both of us.

This workplace did not possess the same quality of comfort or humanity that I'd felt in my previous jobs. We were there to support our artists and to keep our collectors happy. Those seemed to be the only two rules.

When Eric Garner was murdered via choke hold by plainclothes detectives on Staten Island on July 17, 2014, I'd been an employee at the gallery for only ten days. Being Black in America is frequently measured against the proximity of death—Christina Sharpe writes beautifully about this in her essential book *In the Wake: On Blackness and Being*.

About three weeks after Garner's murder, I should have been more prepared for the Saturday that I learned of Michael Brown's extrajudicial execution under similar circumstances. My father's side of the family is from Missouri, but I had never heard of Ferguson before the news screened videos of Brown's dead body lying at the scene of the crime. Brown lay blood-soaked in the hot street for hours. My heart sank.

I left my desk to take a walk, but as I made my way to the exit, I began to cry.

I looked around, and it was still just a regular Saturday for everyone else. I didn't think much of it until a few days had passed, and it was just another Tuesday, followed by just another Wednesday. It was as if Ferguson wasn't a reality for my coworkers. Granted, you're not "supposed" to talk about religion or politics at work, but police aren't "supposed" to murder unarmed Black people, either. The rules I knew suddenly stopped making sense.

With Brown's death, we entered an era on social media with frequent updates from grassroots organizers in the streets of Ferguson. There was an intimacy and invitation provided by voices on social media urging us to stay vigilant, not only with respect to Brown's murder, but to the way the police treat peaceful protestors. As the artist Dread Scott shared in an opinion piece for the Walker Art Center, "The only reason we are talking about the murder of Michael

Brown today is because people stood up and stayed in the streets. In the face of increasing violence from various police forces, the only response is stepping up the struggle for justice."

In the days following the deaths, images by photographers and other witnesses began to define a resurfacing justice movement for Black victims of police brutality. Though my workplace was utterly unchanged by the moment, my community responded in full force, trying to make sense of it all through their creative and collective work. My faith in the importance of art had never been more concrete. It was images, sculptures, and writing that helped me wade through the anger I was feeling. There was a moment of respite whenever I encountered a work that mirrored feelings that felt too complicated to define on my own.

One night after work, I went to a reading by my dear friend Morgan Parker. She read from her poem "I Feel Most Colored When I am Thrown Against a Sharp White Background: after Glenn Ligon after Zora Neale Hurston":

I am growing two fruits.

I feel most colored when I am thrown against
    the sidewalk.

It is the last time I feel colored.

Stone is the name of the fruit.

I am a man I am a man I am a woman I am
    a man I am a woman I am protected
    and served.

I background my country.

My country sharp in my throat.

I pay taxes and I am a child and I grow into a
    bright fleshy fruit.

White bites: I stain the uniform.

I am thrown black typeface in a headline with
    no name.

Or, no one hears me.

I am thrown a bone, "Unarmed."

I feel most colored when my weapon is I.

When I get what I deserve.

When I can't breathe.

Hearing Morgan read her poem for the first time,
I wept. It feels dramatic to say, but the tears felt like a

battle cry for the strong person I needed to become at that point in my life, in my career, and for my growing audience. The tears helped me liberate the part of myself that I was afraid to be. A part of myself that I thought I had to hide.

Later that year, Americans witnessed the murder of John Crawford III at a Walmart, Akai Gurley in New York City's Pink Houses, Laquan McDonald, and twelve-year-old Tamir Rice, killed right before his sister's eyes. Every opportunity to heal the wound was met with extreme violence and disappointment.

On December 5, 2014, I posted a call for art in support of the #BlackLivesMatter movement on Black Contemporary Art. The page, which still exists on the blog, links to work that was selected by our editors or submitted by our community. It was developed as a space for collective healing and mourning—for anyone who needed to experience art that attempted to offer sense in this tumultuous time. In that moment, I began to understand how intimately art and activism could work together to produce a collective voice and shared community. And for me, there was no going back.

When I learned that my friend Lucy Redoglia would be leaving her role as the Metropolitan Museum of Art's associate online community producer, I had a gut feeling that I needed to apply to be her successor. I knew I had the qualifications, but I had some sincere doubts about working at the Met. Before I could figure it out, I joined a group called Museum Hue for their tour of the Met with Sandra Jackson-Dumont, the museum's chairman of education.

Sandra was unlike any other museum person I'd ever met. She warmly greeted each guard and spoke loudly as we walked toward the information desk to begin the tour. In her opening remarks, she listed off her illustrious résumé, citing work at the Seattle

Art Museum and the Studio Museum in Harlem. She spoke candidly about how she'd shifted the culture of each of the institutions she'd chosen to work with, and then finally began to speak about the Met. She asserted that she had very clear goals in her career and that the Met was not the exact definition of success for her. She had other models for success that she had defined on her own terms. Hearing her speak left me feeling emotional, and by the end of her hour-long tour, I was in tears, moved by the spirit of her ownership.

Meeting Sandra helped me answer some of the lingering questions I had about working at the Met and working in the arts in general. She helped me keep sight of the fact that I could set my own benchmarks and expect accountability. She assured everyone on the tour that we don't have to subscribe to anyone else's idea of success. I sent in my application that week.

My journey at the Metropolitan Museum of Art began on July 6, 2015. I laughed to myself as I walked down Madison Avenue and saw a crew of art handlers delivering a multimillion-dollar John Chamberlain sculpture. I was far away from the world of my upbringing and walking headstrong into a gilded, elitist paradise.

At that point in my career, I knew I'd earned my spot, but I still fielded a lot of *weird* energy that summer. I'd met a former guard who, upon meeting me, said, "The Met hired someone *like you*." I remember offhand remarks from my department head about how I didn't dress like anyone else at the museum. I took them in stride. I did not want to be like everyone else at the museum. I loved wearing glitter-covered sneakers and letting my locs bounce around as I went from meeting to meeting. I didn't want to fit in. I also didn't want the museum to be monolithic in that way.

My favorite thing about the Met was that it always felt like a building full of stories. The Metropolitan Museum of Art doesn't have a *Mona Lisa*, or a singular famous work of art, like the Musée du Louvre. The Met is home to so many masterpieces from so many different cultures; there is something for anyone who wants to visit.

As the years carried on, I used this optimism as a shield. I wielded it when people expressed surprise that someone *like me* sauntered proudly through the museum's halls. The optimism came to my defense whenever I spotted one of the museum's many flaws. Optimism kept me afloat as I set out to fix them.

As a social media maven, I was granted the opportunity to tell so many of the museum's stories, but also project the museum that I wanted the world to see. The museum that we could be if we thought more inclusively and abundantly.

On February 28, 2016, a Sunday, I did a lecture alongside the artist Christine Sun Kim. Our presentation focused on the concepts of feedback and noise for the Bruce High Quality Foundation, a Brooklyn arts collective. On the day of the program, I went first and took a relatively unorthodox approach, discussing online sex chat rooms, the photographer Carla Williams, and the musicians Missy Elliott and Janet Jackson. I didn't really want to give a super narrow "fine art" history lecture. I wanted to do something sexier that felt more at home for me and the way my brain worked. That, and I can't think of the word *feedback* without starting to sing Janet's 2007 song "Feedback." Truly a gift.

Next, Christine, accompanied by a sign language interpreter, spoke about her own voice and shared illustrations of her research on sound and communication. Christine is a sound-based artist who is also deaf. In partnering with Christine, I realized that I had never thought to have interpreters or live-captioning at any of my lectures. I was and still am totally blown away by Christine's super-genius brain.

I am thankful to her for both her artwork and for the inadvertent wake-up call she gave me. There is still more work to be done to open doors to people who are not readily welcomed into the art world.

After that talk, I became ever more obsessed with thinking about who was not in the room during my conversations at work. Unfortunately, because I was working at the Met, there was a lack of diversity in almost all of my meetings with respect to disability, socioeconomic status, race, etc. It made me feel feral some days.

I became obsessed with the Met's steps. As social media manager, I'd track Instagram updates that showed young people perched on the steps re-creating scenes from the show *Gossip Girl*. If you open the museum's geotag on Instagram, nearly half of the images are of people posing on the steps. Millions of people tune into Met Gala coverage of people walking up the museum's steps! What are the real-world consequences when one of the museum's most iconic spaces is inaccessible for so many? What happens when people aren't told that, less than a block away, there's an accessible entrance? Could social media be a viable medium for making the museum more welcoming to disabled visitors? What could I actually do?

For three years, with the power of social media, I tried to show as many people as possible how many doors there could be to the institution. At that time, my own star began to rise, as well. I welcomed every opportunity for more visibility as a chance to spread the gospel of inclusion. At work, I partnered with the museum's Access Coordination team to highlight the programming it provided for disabled visitors. One of my proudest moments was doing Facebook Live tours of exhibitions in American Sign Language, Spanish, and Korean in an effort to enrich the museum's largely English-oriented online program.

But something was still missing for me. Each day that I walked into the building, I would see busts of Bramante, Michelangelo, Raphael, Dürer, Rembrandt, and Velázquez carved into the building's façade by the sculptor Karl Bitter. I thought about how I may never see Carrie Mae Weems, Loïs Mailou Jones, or

Jacob Lawrence celebrated in the same way. I knew I was changing the Met, but I also knew in my heart that all of that effort could be better utilized at a grassroots level.

At the end of my three years at the Met, I knew it was time to take what I'd learned elsewhere. I needed the agency to make my own decisions about who and how I wanted to be in the world. I wanted to have a voice in the art world. Only this time, I wanted it on my own terms.

Before I began writing, I thought about the sensation I felt when I listened to Solange Knowles's song "Mad" from *A Seat at the Table*. The song begins with Solange's layered vocals harmonizing "You got the right to be mad." It feels a little like a gospel, something more akin to ancient scripture than R&B or pop music. In this book, I had a personal goal of writing a tribute to my anger. I wanted to share a few moments that have shaped me as an activist and as a proudly angry Black person who has loved art for as long as they can remember. There was a point in my career where I feared my anger. I feared that my anger would scare others. But looking back, I know without a doubt that I have the right to be mad—

on these pages and out in the world.

This being true, on the other hand, my story is not wholeheartedly about anger and could never be. My story is also about generosity. It's about the things that artists and friends teach us and how we employ them in our own lives. My story was catapulted by whoever approved my application at the Studio Museum, by every follower of my blog, and by the brilliant people I've met throughout my journey. Now, I do my best to pay that forward. We don't have to be at the end of our careers to uplift others; we must uplift one another along the way if we are to survive.

In creative fields, when it comes to a lack of diversity, many blame "the pipeline." They claim that a lack of applicants inhibits them from making more inclusive hiring decisions. I refuse to believe that, and I want you to know that I see you and thank you. I have seen many rooms that need people just like you. Please, never ever hesitate to begin your own journey into the arts. From the outside, you may see the same names inscribed as I did when I looked at the Met's facade. They may intimidate you, too. I hope you also know that if we're ever going to add to the list of names that are celebrated in history, we'll be stronger together.

Protest is way more complicated than communicating rage. Small actions foster change. Our activism, like any other part of ourselves, develops into something bigger than a singular experience. Activism is a collective action and an investment in the lives of other people. And, as the late artist Thornton Dial once said, "If there is one thing that you can do, leave something for somebody else . . . You can work for somebody else's freedom. You can leave something for somebody else's child."

So, like I said, this is not your traditional text about art, protest, or anger by an established scholar. This is my story about loving art so much that you want to see it change for the better. That is what I know, above all.

ABOUT US

Pocket Change Collective was born out of a need for space. Space to think. Space to connect. Space to be yourself. And this is your invitation to join us.

These books are small, but they are mighty. They ask big questions and propose even bigger solutions. They show us that no matter where we come from or where we're going, we can all take part in changing the communities around us. Because the possibilities of how we can use our space for good are endless.

So thank you. Thank you for picking this book up. Thank you for reading. Thank you for being a part of the Pocket Change Collective.